One of the outstanding Biblical scholars and Christian theologians of his generation, Dr. Robinson has written in *The Cross of Hosea* a book for everyone who seeks in the Bible vital truth for life today. The nature of God, the inwardness of sin, and the victory of grace — these great themes are illuminated with fresh insight against the background of Hosea's experience with his adulterous wife Gomer.

This experience is shown to have led directly to Hosea's revolutionary concept of God's love and its meaning for human beings. "We have here," writes Dr. Robinson, "a supreme example of the place of experience in the prophetic consciousness, and of the warp of human life on the loom of Scripture, across which the shuttle of the Spirit of God so constantly moved." The process of revelation is seen to be, not a mere mechanical process that shows a truth existing externally to man, but a process that operates in and through human experience.

While clarifying the relation between Hosea's personal experience and the new truths that he perceived, Dr. Robinson emphasizes the significance of the truths themselves, and points

After six years in the ministry, he became professor of Church history and the philosophy of religion at Rawdon College, Leeds. For twenty-two years he was Principal of Regent's Park College, Oxford, and Principal Emeritus until his death in 1945.

He served as examiner in both theology and Hebrew at many of Britain's leading universities, including Oxford, Edinburgh, Wales, and Liverpool. Author of many books, he was awarded the Birkett Medal for Biblical Studies by the British Academy.

THE
CROSS OF HOSEA

THE
CROSS OF HOSEA

By H. Wheeler Robinson

Edited by Ernest A. Payne

PHILADELPHIA
THE WESTMINSTER PRESS

In the last resort, it is in the prophetic consciousness and its continuance in personal religion that there is found the ultimate sanctuary in which the voice of God is still heard, the sanctuary in which the ancient Scriptures are still transferred into His living oracles."

H. W. R.

CONTENTS

THE
CROSS OF HOSEA

THE MARRIAGE OF HOSEA

THE chief thing that Bacon had to say about love was that " it troubleth men's fortunes "; and about marriage: " He that hath wife and children hath given hostages to fortune." Had he thought with understanding of the Prophet Hosea he might have enlarged his horizon toward that of another famous essayist. Emerson, writing on *Compensation,* adds the necessary complement concerning the gain that may lie in a man's apparent loss. " Whilst he sits on the cushion of advantages, he goes to sleep. When he is pushed, tormented, defeated, he has a chance to learn something." The sorrows of Hosea were his " chance of the prize of learning love."

How love might be, hath been indeed, and is;

so that his " soul's prowess " came to lie in his faithful answer to " life's proof ":

Does God love,
And will ye hold that truth against the world?

Yet, as Emerson so emphatically asserts, this law of reciprocity does not work mechanically in the spiritual realm; it is the evil to which we do not succumb that is a benefactor. True as that is of our common humanity, it is especially true of a prophet, and of such a prophet as Hosea, whose call lay in his experience, and whose experience was made by his own attitude to the events which befell him. Even in that ancient world, so remote from our modernity, his theology was " the theology of experience."

The modern interest in the psychology of religious experience, combined with critical study of the records of Hebrew prophets, has led to a great deal of attention being given to their inner life and thought. This is well worth-while, both for exegesis and for theology in general, though the lack of information about their outer life and circumstances usually leaves our results somewhat uncertain in detail. Their lives were so subordinated to their messages that it is often only through those messages that we can reconstruct their lives. This fact makes the story of Hosea's marriage the more important, for here, if anywhere, we may see the outer event shaping the inner experience, and its resultant expression in the prophet's " thus saith the Lord."

The account of the marriage of Hosea is contained in the first and the third chapters of the collection of oracles bearing his name. According to the first chapter, Hosea is commanded to take a harlot for his wife, and children of harlotry; he accordingly marries Gomer bath-Diblaim, who subsequently has three children, to whom the prophet gives symbolic names, which become the texts of prophetic messages concerning Israel. According to the third chapter, Hosea is commanded to love an unnamed woman, loved by a paramour, and an adultress. He obeys by purchasing her, apparently from some kind of undescribed servitude, and by setting her apart for what seems to be a probationary period. These are practically all our facts, and anything else is an interpretation of them, justified or unjustifiable.

1. *The Actual Events*

The first point we have to decide is this — did these events actually happen, or are they an allegory by which the unfaithfulness of Israel to Yahweh might be the more vividly set forth? I have no hesitation at all in regarding them as real events, issuing from the sex relation of man and woman, though the two chapters mingle interpretation with event in what to us is a somewhat confusing way. It is not necessary to suppose that Hosea married a woman whom he knew at the time to be unchaste. The terms of the narrative may simply mean that when the prophet did interpret his own life prophetically in the light of after events as being under the providential guidance of God, he saw that he had, in fact, though unconsciously at the time, taken to himself a woman *destined* to be a wife of harlotry and to bear children of harlotry. This seems more likely than that the prophet knowingly married a woman of unchaste spirit or conduct, though such a supposition could not in itself be excluded as impossible. The symbolical acts of the Hebrew prophets, such as Isaiah's walking about Jerusalem for three years in the dress of a captive slave, are often strange to us, and are explicable only by the completeness of surrender to the prophetic impulse. But it is more natural to suppose that a discovery of Gomer's infidelity was made subsequently, and that the story of the first chapter has been written down (not necessarily by the prophet himself) from this subsequent standpoint. We have a parallel to this prophetic interpretation of an actual event which happened independently of it, in the symbolic meaning which Ezekiel gives to his wife's death (Ezek. 24: 15 ff.) , when he abstains from the usual mourning customs to symbolize the effect of the fall of Jerusalem upon the people. We have another example in Jeremiah's purchase of family property at Anathoth, of which the symbolic significance emerges only after the event (Jer. 32: 7). In further support of the view that Hosea's marriage was an actual event allegorically interpreted, and not an invented allegory, we may notice such details as the name of Gomer, and the weaning of her daughter, or the details about the purchase price of the unnamed woman in the third chapter, which have no significance for allegory at all.

A more difficult question to decide concerns the relation of the third chapter to the first. Is it sequel, parallel, or prelude? The prevalent, and the prima facie natural view, is that the third chapter is the sequel to the first, the intervening chapter making the allegorical application of the first. According to this view, the unnamed woman of the third chapter is still Gomer of the first. But in the interval, she must be supposed to have left her husband and to have passed into other hands — those of a private owner, or possibly of a temple, at which she may be serving as one of the " religious " prostitutes of the time. We are not told directly of this separation, at least in the present records of Hosea's life and ministry, any more than we are told what actually happened after the period of probation. But we are given to understand that Hosea intends to take Gomer back to his home when she is ready for it. The second view — that the third chapter is parallel to the first — is based chiefly on the arguments that the important fact of Gomer's departure from her husband ought not to be left to the imagination; that Gomer would have been definitely named or indicated, if this were a sequel; and that the narrative of the third chapter is in the first person, i.e., autobiographic, whilst that of the first is in the third person, i.e., biographic, a fact which is taken to suggest that they come from different hands, describing in different ways the prophet's one and only marriage. The third view, that chapter 3 gives us Hosea's own account of events *preceding* his marriage, has been more recently advocated. According to this, Hosea knowingly married a woman of unchaste character, who was openly living with a paramour, but did this only after a period of probation. He tells us this in the third chapter, written at a time when the marriage had not taken place, and the children of the first chapter accordingly had not yet been born. We are informed of these subsequent events by a later biographer, and may infer that the adultery of Gomer took place after the birth of the first child. It is alleged that we have no further knowledge of Hosea's marriage experience than is given in chapter 1, and therefore no ground in it for ascribing optimistic prophecies to the prophet, as his final word. The hopeful period came earlier in his life, whilst he still thought that Gomer might be successfully redeemed from sin.

Obviously, the more romantic story is that of the first view — that Hosea seeks to reclaim the fallen Gomer at the end, and not at the beginning. But we must not allow the attraction of this "romance," or its greater theological suggestiveness, to sway our exegesis. Our first duty is to decide, on grounds of literary criticism, which is the more probable view, and only then to test this by its larger relations. Of the three views, the third seems to me least probable and most arbitrary, and it involves emendation of the text in the interests of a theory. It throws the emphasis of the prophet on the reclamation of a woman who has not been faithless to *him*, instead of on that of a faithless wife who has borne at least one child of which he is the father. It presupposes a double unchastity, and confuses the allegorical application. The second view, that the difference of the narratives is due to their being by different hands, and that they give an inside and outside account of the same events, is difficult to maintain, because the events are not the same. In the first chapter Hosea is bidden to take an unchaste woman, in the third to love an adulterous woman. In the first, the births of three children are described in succession, in a way that implies the passage of at least five years; in the third, a woman is bought for a slave's price, and put into isolation for " many days." The two narratives seem irreconcilable, if they are to be regarded as parallel accounts of Hosea's marriage. Certainly, no one would be likely to refer them to the same set of incidents, unless as an escape from greater difficulties. But it is hard to see why we should not take chapters 1 and 3 in their present order as parts of a prophetical narrative referring to different periods of Hosea's life. They may not both be written by the prophet; indeed, the change of person from the third to the first suggests this; and it is more natural to regard the first chapter as giving a report by a biographer, which more or less faithfully reflects the earlier life of Hosea; whilst, in the third chapter, we have a fragment of later autobiography from the prophet himself. There are many parallels in the prophetical books, e.g., in Jeremiah, to this interchange of biography and autobiography. The fact that Gomer is not named in the third chapter means nothing if " a woman beloved of her paramour and an adulteress " is a sufficient characterization of her, as it would be if she had been unfaithful to Hosea in the course of their married life. It is true that we have to infer this fact from the first description of

her, as " a wife of harlotry "; but this applies to all other theories which seek a basis for the allegory in real events. We have always to remember the allusive character of such writing; no more is named than the writer or speaker requires at the moment. We would not have heard that Ezekiel was married, had he not been led to make his wife's funeral a symbol of the national tragedy.

In the present arrangement of the first three chapters there is an intelligible order. We have, first, the marriage followed by the births of three children, with the suggestion of their mother's infidelity to her husband. We have, in the second chapter, the allegorical application of these events: " Plead with your mother, plead; for she is not my wife, neither am I her husband," says Yahweh to the people of the land, i.e., its children, who are " children of harlotry " (Hos. 2: 2 ff.) . This condemnation passes into the promise of a new betrothal of Israel to Yahweh, with new and permanent qualities, and a reversal of the old condemnatory names of the children. This latter part of the chapter obviously runs into the ground of the real experience of the prophet in the following chapter; his love persists, in spite of the infidelity, and is interpreted as a divine command to win back his faithless wife to better ways. The experiential text of the sermon found in the second chapter therefore lies in the first and third chapters, taken in this sequence; but the preacher reserves the closing part of his text till the sermon is concluded, when it becomes a human illustra tion of the divine truth. There are difficulties enough in the oracles of Hosea without exaggerating those of th opening chapters. We may, therefore, remain conter with the ordinary view of the events of Hosea's ma riage, with which many Old Testament scholars are st

satisfied; the chief fault to find with it seems to be that it has lost the charm of novelty. On the other hand, if sound in itself, it does supply a ground for regarding Hosea as not finally a pessimist as to his nation, and for ascribing to him the oracles which are promises, as well as those which are warnings and condemnations.

2. *The Application to Religion*

The justification for this discussion of Hosea's marriage is that it has important results not only for exegesis, but also for theology. In regard to exegesis, a careful study of The Book of Hosea would show how deeply the oracles which it contains are colored by the experience of his marriage; how frequently the figure of marital infidelity enters into them; how warm is the feeling with which the relation of Yahweh to Israel is described; how passionate is the longing of God portrayed in them to betroth a faithful people to himself. We may not feel warranted in relating all the oracles to this one series of events as closely and comprehensively as some have done; but there can be little doubt that the chief psychological explanation of the oracles is derived from Hosea's relations with Gomer. It may even be that the bitterness of the prophet's attack on the immorality of the high places and of the priests connected with them is due to a personal element — that it was from one of these sanctuaries that he had, in the literal sense, to redeem the temple prostitute Gomer, because she had first been led astray by the licensed sexuality of their festivals, and had left her husband for professional connection with a sanctuary.

There is certainly a depth of personal emotion in this book which can be paralleled nowhere else save in the

greater prophet so like Hosea — Jeremiah — who knew the sorrows of a lonely and threatened life, as Hosea did those of an unhappy marriage. But our present concern is not with the detailed exegesis of The Book of Hosea, but with its theological significance. He is the first to make a profoundly ethical application of the figure of marriage to the relation between God and man. Of course, the sex element had taken a great place in primitive religion, including the Canaanite. The mystery of sex, like the mystery of blood, was an inevitable feature in early interpretation of the comprehensive mystery of life, and of its relation to the superhuman powers surrounding man and his existence. The conception of the god as physically married to the land and as producing its fruits seems part of the idea underlying the fertility cults (cf. ch. 1: 2). But the moral side of the sex relation, the higher principles which lead to its sublimation in human experience, and may make human love the most divine of all man's experiences, because the most fully reflecting the love of God, and preparing man to understand and respond to it — all this great line of thought which culminates in the gospel of the New Testament was initiated by Hosea. We see it already working in the Jewish interpretation of the Song of Songs as an allegory of the history of Israel, the bride of Yahweh, from the Exodus to the final restoration of all things. An anthology of love lyrics, containing nothing that is religious at all in the ordinary sense, was thus raised to what a Jewish rabbi called the Holy of Holies of Israel's sacred literature. We know how profoundly the figure has affected Christian thought and its devotional vocabulary, from Saint Paul's comparison of marriage with the relation of Christ and the Church onwards. Hosea is the first begetter of all this line of thought, and he holds this

19

place because of the actual experiences of his life, prophetically interpreted.

We have here, then, a supreme example of the place of experience in the prophetic consciousness, and of the warp of human life on the loom of Scripture, across which the shuttle of the Spirit of God so constantly moved. We are reminded here, at the beginning of Israel's higher conceptions of God that revelation lies in and through that unity of religious experience in which the human and the divine personality lose their " otherness." In the prophetic consciousness, which is one of the noblest kinds of religious consciousness, all is human, and all is divine. These things have been made familiar to us by historical criticism of the Bible, but it cannot be said that their full theological consequences for a doctrine of revelation have yet been recognized.

A sound doctrine of revelation really raises the issues of the incarnation itself — the fundamental kinship of human and divine personality. So long as revelation is regarded as the communication to man of a truth about God already existing externally to the man himself, *in that form,* so long the process remains mechanical; and reduces man to a mere amanuensis, as Calvin indeed held. But when we see that the revelation is made in and through a human experience, in which experience the truth to be revealed is first created, *in that form,* we are ready to face the implication of this, viz., that human experience *is* capable of representing the divine. There will of course be all kinds of limitation due to man's imperfection, mental and moral, and we must suppose a divine kenosis in God's acceptance of these limitations for his purpose — a kenosis as real in its way as that described by the Apostle Paul in regard to the eternal Son of God. But if the love of Hosea for his faithless wife does really represent, in spite of its human limitations, the love of God for Israel; if the word "love," in fact, is to be allowed any human connotation at all in regard to God, it must be because the human personality is in some sense akin to the divine (cf. ch. 11: 4) though far below it (ch. 11: 9). Moreover, the revelation is made through the unity of fellowship between God and man and is born of their intercourse.

The prophets doubtless interpreted the message as coming from without, in accord with their general psychology. They saw visions of external happenings; heard voices, as with their physical ears; felt the hand of Yahweh upon them in quasi-physical compulsions. But all these features belong to their own interpretation of the psychical events, and we may describe them in different terms without injustice to the events themselves or their divine significance as "revelation." The sorrowful experience of Hosea as a man and not as a prophet, might have had no such significance, however warm his affection for Gomer, and however loyal his endeavor to raise her from shame. The new fact is made when Hosea, the prophet, reinterprets this experience as having such significance, and makes the prophetic "venture of faith" in saying that this is how God sorrows and God loves. He could not make this venture unless he implicitly believed that God's nature was somehow like his own. No doubt he does not explicitly put it like this; in fact, he represents Yahweh as saying, " I am God and not man." The transcendence of God is explicit; the immanence of God is implicit. But the whole revelation through prophecy rests on the assumption that human experience and thought *can* reveal God, which means that there is no fundamental unlikeness between the human and the divine personality.

3. *The Higher Anthropomorphism*

This assumption, which we may call " the higher an-thropomorphism," has its negative side in the prophetic attitude toward idolatry, first revealed in Hosea him-self (ch. 8: 4 ff.). Just as they felt that the inner con-sciousness of man and his outer experience in history could and did reveal God, so they felt that the material representation of him in wood and metal and stone could not reveal him. The human medium of revela-tion was not only infinitely higher, but was itself dy-namic and ever moving onward, so as to be capable of becoming more and more adequate to the unveiling of the living God. The material medium was not only in-comparably inferior to the human consciousness, since it was the mere semblance of lifeless flesh, but it was once and for all time fixed and static. Carry forward these two lines of revelation — the spiritual and the ma-terial — and you come logically to the contrast between the revelation in the Prophet of Nazareth, and that in the Torah, supposed to have been given in its perfection and all-sufficiency by Moses, which imprisons the revela-tion of God in the letter of the Law. The religion of the incarnation continues the religion of the prophets, not only in moral and religious teaching, but also in implicit theology. The prophetic emphasis on the human con-science as the most adequate revelation of God is the true forerunner and anticipation of the prologue to the Fourth Gospel: " The law was given by Moses; grace and truth came by Jesus Christ."

4. The Passibility of God

This leads to the question of the doctrine of the passibility of God, the ascription of sorrow and suffering to him. Dr. J. K. Mozley, in *The Impassibility of God* (The Macmillan Company, 1926), has virtually confined himself to an historical record, pointing out the marked contrast between ancient and modern Christian thought on this subject. Until the Reformation, and indeed after it, there was "a steady and continuous, if not quite unbroken, tradition in Christian theology as to the freedom of the divine nature from all suffering and from any potentiality of suffering" (p. 127). In modern theology, on the other hand, there has been a strong reaction against the doctrine of impassibility, represented by such theologians as Bushnell, Fairbairn, Streeter, and Archbishop Temple; and by such Christian philosophers as Lotze and Pringle-Pattison. The last-named claims that the open secret of the universe is, "a God who lives in the perpetual giving of Himself, who shares in the life of His finite creatures, bearing in them and with them the whole burden of their finitude, their sinful wanderings and sorrows, and the suffering without which they cannot be made perfect" (*The Idea of God,* Oxford University Press, 1917, p. 411). Professor H. R. Mackintosh says, in *The Christian Experience of Forgiveness* (Harper & Brothers, 1927, p. 218), "Ideas of the Divine impassibility derived from ages which were very far from humane, and which too often regarded suffering unconcernedly as a mark of the weak and the vanquished, can now make little appeal." On the other hand, we have such a study as the late Baron von Hügel's *Suffering and*

God, published in the second series of his *Essays,* in which he contends that whilst men sin and suffer, and Christ suffers but does not sin, there is as little room for suffering as for sin in God, who is pure Joy. This essay seems to me quite wrong in its contention that the prophets of Israel did not attribute suffering to God (p. 186), and that what they say is to be dismissed as imagery. Let us apply that contention to one of the most moving passages in The Book of Hosea (ch. 11: 8, 9):

How shall I give thee up, Ephraim?
How shall I hand thee over, Israel?
How shall I give thee up as Admah, set thee as Zeboim?
My heart is turned upon me,
My compassions are kindled together;
I will not carry out my hot anger,
I will not again destroy Ephraim.

If we say that this expresses only a passionless " sympathy," and that God does not sorrow and does not suffer because of the sin of his people, how much force is left in such words? How can a God who is *apathetic* be also *sympathetic?* But if Hosea's words are interpreted by that experience of the prophet in which they seem to have arisen — Hosea's own inability to detach himself from Gomer because of his sorrowing and suffering love for her — then the words become charged with a gospel, and point on directly to the truths of the New Testament. We may indeed ask how there can be " sympathy " at all without suffering? If sympathy be a " feeling with " the sufferer, is not that very feeling itself a form of suffering? If the love of God is more than a metaphor, must not the suffering of God be as real, though with all the qualifications in both love and suffering which come

24

from the reference to God instead of man? It seems a dangerous thing to dismiss such sayings as imagery, unless we go on to admit quite frankly that all human language about God is but symbolic, though not the less capable of symbolizing ultimate truths. The danger is continued in the realm of Christology, when with Von Hügel and many others we say that Christ suffered as man, but not as God. Somehow that distinction, however convenient to the theologian, does not seem to ring true to the story of the Gospels, or to the strong language of The Epistle to the Hebrews about the suffering of the Son of God.

The final joy of God must be beyond question; the Christian conception of God cannot be of a worn and anxious and burdened traveler, fearful lest he may not reach his world goal. God is a burden bearer, according to the Hebrew prophets (Isa. 46: 3, 4), but it is because he carries *willingly* the burden of his people. He is, as a later Jewish teacher said, "forever young," and his triumph is no uncertain thing in a universe of risks. But the Christian conception seems to be that of a triumph through the cross, a victory through apparent defeat, a joy that is all the richer joy because it is won, like that of Jesus, through great suffering, voluntarily accepted and endured for the joy that was set before him. The conception of a God who cannot suffer makes theology much more manageable, but leaves it high and dry, like the gods of the Epicureans:

> . . . who haunt
> The lucid interspace of world and world,
> Where never creeps a cloud, or moves a wind,
> Nor ever falls the least white star of snow,
> Nor ever lowest roll of thunder moans,

25

Nor sound of human sorrow mounts to mar
Their sacred everlasting calm!

5. *The Relation to Historical Revelation*

Finally, it is in place to notice here the relation of such
an experience as Hosea's to the whole validity of an historical revelation; that is, the adequacy of a revelation
of the infinite God in and through finite events. Both
Judaism and Christianity are committed to such events;
eliminate the Exodus and Sinai, eliminate the cross and
the resurrection, and you change the very essence of
both religions, and their faith that God is ever active
and that he is known by what he does in history. What
do we lose when we play with the idea that we may re-
tain the ideas of the Gospel and not concern ourselves
with the question as to what actually happened in history? I cannot express it better than Dr. H. G. Wood
has done, in his book, *Christianity and the Nature of
History:* " While all the ideal values may remain if you
impugn the historic record set forth in the gospels, these
ideal values are not certified to the common man as
inherent in the very nature of things " (p. 28) . It is that
note of actuality which is common to the whole revelation in the Bible, and to a prophetic experience such as
Hosea's in particular. It was one thing to hold in general
that God loved Israel; it was another to have that confirmed by the analogy of his own experience, and to
know that God *so* loved Israel, as Hosea found himself
loving Gomer. The experience both confirmed the idea
and enlightened it by bringing a new standard of meas-
urement to its appreciation. The love of God could not
be less than the love of man, so the love of man became
a pledge and a revelation of the love of God.

THE INWARDNESS OF SIN

THE characteristic of God is grace; the characteristic of man in his present stage of development is sin, the production of which is the proof of his highest attribute, that is, his freedom to act even in rebellion against God. Now it is one of the tendencies of modern preaching, as of modern hearing, to take God's grace for granted as something that is self-evident and to dismiss any emphasis on man's sin as rather in the nature of a theological fiction. This attitude altogether ignores the fact that all of us know a great deal about sin from our direct experience, whereas we know the grace of God only at the circumference of his being where it touches our life. It is quite true that sin is a theological term and that it denotes the religious aspect of moral evil. In the strict sense of the word, there can be no sin where there is no religion, but the substance and content of sin, that is, moral evil, belong to the undeniable experience of all of us, and all of us know a great deal about it, far more in fact than we know about God's grace. When we turn to the masterpieces of literature, it will not be long before we are faced with some adequate recognition of this truth as a rebuke to our superficial neglect of it. Let us take, for example, one of the great studies of sin which Shakespeare has given us, viz., *Macbeth,* and see if it does not reveal certain permanent and universal characteristics of moral evil, whether we call it sin or not.

In the first place, a study of *Macbeth* can teach us that

sin is that which it does. We see the evil of it in its consequences, both within and without; in the surrender of a nature capable of great things to the power of superstition, to the denial of all honor and loyalty, to deed after deed of cruelty and wrong, till the sinner is left alone and helpless, hating the very life that he has made for himself.

In the second place, sin, like righteousness, is nurtured socially. It would often shrink with horror from itself as it begins to see its own consequences, if it were not for the spur and encouragement of other sinners. Evil, like good, needs the momentum of other lives to be added to itself in order to achieve its full power and reveal its true nature. Macbeth, without his wife, would never have done his first deed of evil. On the other hand, Banquo's fellowship might have saved him from it. But the heart gathers its own society and by the momentum of that society becomes capable of the worst.

In the third place, however close this dependence of sin on social environment and fellowship, sin begins within, long before that outer occasion and opportunity which is often called temptation. It begins, in the case of Macbeth, in the unbridled ambition, the lust for self-glory, the dwelling on the thought of selfish ends, till evil aims are designed to gratify the lust and the heart is ready for its external opportunity. This emphasis on the inwardness of sin which is so conspicuous in Shakespeare's study of Macbeth is in no degree cancelled by his recognition of the weird sisters as a point of contact with the supernatural world. They are, after all, merely an extension of Macbeth's social environment, a supernatural parallel to Lady Macbeth herself, in the natural order, and their presence and action do not in the least exonerate Macbeth. They do not lead Banquo astray.

In the fourth place, sin is shown to be doomed by its intrinsic character. It creates its own penalties, alienating the good which might have brought deliverance from it, hardening itself to worse and worse deeds which dispense with even the poor excuse of its own beginning. Sooner or later, it finds the universe arrayed against it; for sin is the challenge to the whole of things by the individual man, which is the sheerest and uttermost folly. Sin ends by destroying the sinner. Granville-Barker rightly sees this in Macbeth and his wife (*A Companion to Shakespeare Studies,* The Macmillan Company, 1934, pp. 79, 82) : " The ebbing of the life within these two, their death while they still live; for here is the essential tragedy . . . in the sleep-walking scene we see her already spiritually dead . . . the man's living spirit does seem at last to shrivel to a cipher . . . he too is dead before he dies."

The student of Macbeth will find all these things set out in the concrete terms of human character and destiny without any suggestion of theology. They recur in the study of every human life, in greater or less degree, though entangled with the veils and disguises of the daily routine which it is the dramatist's business to strip off. Certainly they may be found by the student of The Book of Hosea; in our study of the theology of sin as here represented, we shall find the same four aspects of sin presented not less definitely even if in obscurer terms, because of the remoter vehicle of expression, i.e., that sin is what it does, that it is socially nurtured, that it begins within, and that it is self-destructive.

1. Hosea's Personal Experience of Moral Evil

It was Hosea's personal experience of moral evil in Gomer, his wife, that gave him, at the cost of so much suffering, such insight into the nature and activity of sin. Thornton Wilder in his little play, *The Angel That Troubled the Waters,* gives the plea of one who seeks for healing in vain, saying, " It is no shame to boast to an Angel of what I might still do in Love's service were I freed from his bondage." To this the angel's reply is: " Without your wound, where would your power be? The very angels themselves cannot persuade the wretched and blundering children on earth as can one human being broken in the wheels of living." Hosea's power was in his wound. He saw that sin spoiled life, both in its quality and in its relations. By his intimate knowledge of what Gomer's infidelity meant to himself, he entered into a new sympathy with the God who is made to suffer through the sin of man. If it be true that moral evil concerns God, and because he is a holy God involves him in suffering (according to our argument in the discussion of Hosea's marriage) then it is only by our own reaction to the sin of others in holy love that we can understand God's consciousness in that small degree which is possible for man at all.

We may say indeed that only the holy man, in proportion to the degree of his holiness, knows what sin is. This sounds a paradox, yet only because we have such artificial conceptions of what holiness is. If we define it by the Christian standards, which means if we measure it by the holiness of Christ, then its chief and essential attribute is love, and love that inevitably suffers through every contact with moral evil. It suffered the more because it cannot disown its own responsibility for the redemption of the sinner. The last thing that holy love is capable of doing is to stand on one side, saying, " I am holier than thou, and thou in thy sin art no concern of mine." It is this false conception of holiness, this negative idea of freedom from pollution, rather than the positive idea of burden bearing, which makes it difficult for us to realize the true nature of holiness, and, therefore, the true nature of sin. Life contains many realities which can be known only through actual contact with them, or participation in them. It is one thing to treat them speculatively. It is quite another to handle them in real life.

Just as Job was brought from his suffering to an inner knowledge of the truth of innocence and the falsity of contemporary theological theory, so was Hosea, through his unhappy association with Gomer, trained and schooled in the university of life to graduate with such high honors in the knowledge of God and of man. Hosea saw what sin meant when he looked on Gomer corrupted by its vice and entangled in its toils. He imagined further what the sin of Israel must mean to God, and his faith in God's final victory over the evil spirit of Israel was the reflection of his own assurance that his love would conquer the spirit of infidelity in Gomer and win her back to a new betrothal, holy and righteous. His enlightened eyes looked forth from his home to the wider horizon. The moral and religious evils of his day had, for him, thenceforward a new significance. He saw that they sprang from the inner spirit of whoredom, which he had known at close quarters and could now recognize on the larger scale (Hos. 4: 12; 5: 4) . He saw how this moral evil was rooted in social relations, buttressed and defended by the vested interests of kings and princes, priests and prophets, passed on from one generation to another in continuous social solidarity. He saw too that its end was death, except for one divine possibility: that which Browning puts into the mouth of the Pope in *The Ring and the Book* when he conceives that even the archvillain, Guido, might have the true nature of things revealed to him by some sudden blaze of light, as he himself had once seen Naples by a lightning flash. The difference is, however, that Hosea's hope is not like that of most of the prophets, based on catastrophic and eschatological expectations. He believes, rather, that a patient and enduring love, eloquent through its suffering, will at last avail to penetrate to the spirit within and transform its alienation. Is not Guido's last cry itself an appeal to his own so deeply wronged wife: " Pompilia, will you let them murder me? " Hosea's aspiration and his expectation are, for the Christian, the prophecy of that which should be in the fullness of the time.

2. *The Social Environment of Sin*

If we are to see Israel's sin as it met the eyes of Hosea, we must first reconstruct, in imagination, the general background of economic, social, and religious life in those days. We must think of the people generally as living in small towns and villages, their one-roomed houses usually clustered on the slopes of one of the hills of Ephraim. Below would be the village well, to which the women would come morning and evening; at the gate, or in some adjacent spot, the men would meet when they had common business; above the houses, on the hilltop, would be the " high place," the local sanctuary. The majority of the people would be engaged in agricultural work, though by this time some were beginning Israel's future world career of trading, under the guidance of the Canaanites. On the hillside there would be the grapes and olives to tend, and the rock presses in which to trample out their juices; down in the valley grew the wheat and barley, which would have to be carried in due season to the threshing floor, up beside the high place near the hilltop. In the little houses, the oil and the meal would be kept in earthen jars, and supplemented by various fruits; flesh would be eaten only on festival days. Their clothing would be of the simplest — a close-fitting tunic, and an outer cloak, used as a sleeping cover.

The social organization of these village groups was hardly more elaborate than their manner of life. It centered in the family group, over which the father ruled; and in the local assembly of male citizens, under the leadership of the elders. The methods of the wandering desert tribe were largely retained in this simple village community, where all men knew each other's affairs. The king counted for little, except in time of war, or when his agents collected some tax or other. The priest at the high place was much more important, for he could give oracles or advice on practical difficulties; the prophet was a more irregular and occasional factor. The community was controlled by customs, local and national, rather than by formal codes of law; these customs would have to be applied to particular circumstances by the sense of the community, interpreted by the elders. The local assembly was at once judicial, military, and religious; a citizen might be called upon to act in any one of these three capacities, at any time. The religious life of the town or village centered in the high place. There would be found the altar, developed from its primitive form of a rough block of unhewn stone, and, near it, perhaps, some ancient and sacred tree; at any rate, there would be the asherah, a wooden post, and the massebah, a stone pillar, these being survivals of more primitive tree and stone worship. In some cases, there was also the image of Yahweh, the ox being the favorite symbol for him among an agricultural people, because of its strength. To this high place the people of the district, men and women, would flock at the time of the great agricultural festivals, and to a less degree at new moons and Sabbaths; whilst many private visits would be made to the sanctuary by those who brought some gift and wanted some favor. If an animal sacrifice was offered the oldest method was to drain, on the altar, its blood, as belonging to the deity, whilst the family and their friends feasted on the flesh, and so realized communion with their god.

These, then, are the main outlines of life in the Northern Kingdom down to the eighth century. It is easy to see some of the abuses and perils of such a free and unsystematized social life, especially when the influx of new wealth disturbed the former social relationships. In the first place, luxury and extravagance replaced the older simplicity — houses of hewn stone, furniture of ivory, cushions of silk, costly and elaborate dress, the drinking of wine from bowls, the eating of flesh every day, drunkenness and gluttony. The rich turned from the good old simple ways of nomad life, which the puritan Rechabites had maintained for centuries. In the second place, the administration of justice pressed hardly on such as were not represented in the local community. Women who were wives or daughters were protected by their fathers and husbands; but the woman who was a widow had no one naturally bound to speak for her;

and the orphan and the alien were in like condition. The wealthier acquired influence in many ways, and evenhanded justice was harder to get, especially because of the bribery of the judges, in which the wealthier could outbid his fellows. It was a hard thing to be poor in Israel in those days; you might be forced to sell not only your land holding, but yourself as well, into slavery, to get food for your family in some time of famine. In this way the smaller holdings were being absorbed into larger estates, sometimes through sheer economic pressure; at others, perhaps, through such " methods of barbarism " as Ahab had practiced on Naboth. Then, in the third place, the conditions of religion were lamentable. The modes of worship at the high places had been taken over from the Canaanites, with all their furniture, and all their customs. The god of each locality had been called its Baal, or " lord," whom the Canaanites had worshiped as the giver of all the fertility of the district. These various Baalim were honored through what would be reckoned by us the grossest sexual immorality. When Israel dispossessed the Canaanites, it meant that Yahweh was dispossessing their Baalim. What was more natural, then, than that He should become heir to their worship, and be worshiped himself as the local Baal, when his people settled down to agricultural life, and needed a God of agriculture? In this way, then, the older religion of Yahweh was passing out of recognition, and was being transformed from the crude but moral religion of the desert to a more cultured but nonmoral, even immoral, nature worship. Against this triple deterioration, then, the growing luxury, the evident injustice, the flagrant immorality of religion, the prophets Amos and Hosea become the protesting voice of Yahweh himself.

There are, however, certain features of this prophetic condemnation peculiar to Hosea, and with these we are especially concerned. His emphasis falls, much more than that of Amos, on the actual immorality of the cult and of its priests, and he seems to be the first to denounce the idolatry which formed part of the worship of Yahweh. The detached oracles begin (chs. 4 to 5: 7) with the denunciation of the priests. *They* are primarily responsible for the ignorance displayed by the people; they feed on the sin of Israel, since they profit by the sacrificial offerings and their multiplication; they have fallen to the level of the people themselves — " like people, like priest." They are even accused of using the sanctuaries as their base of operations for actual robbery and murder (ch. 6: 9) . The fatal attraction of the cult practiced at the sanctuaries is compared with the hunter's snare and net and pit. No wonder that there is actual whoredom and adultery among the people where such evil things are consecrated as a part of the ritual (ch. 4: 13, 14; the reference is to the fertility rites of Baalism) . The bull images of the sanctuaries are denounced again and again (chs. 2: 8, R.V., margin; 4: 17; 8: 4–6; 9: 6; 10: 5, 10; 11: 2; 13: 2; 14: 3, 8) ; the term " calf " is purposely contemptuous for the small bull images of wood or baser metal plated with silver or gold. These represented the God of Israel as the source of the fertility of the land, as some of them had probably represented the local Baalim, before they were transferred to the cult of Yahweh.

Further, Hosea, is the pioneer of a new attitude toward the monarchy. According to the earlier of the two stories of its inception in The First Book of Samuel (chs. 9; 10: 1–16; 11: 1–11, 15) , the first king was chosen and anointed by Samuel, acting with the full approval and by the inspiration of Yahweh. But the kingship was bound up with the patronage of the cult which the eighth-century prophets had been led to condemn. The rebellion of Jehu against the dynasty of Omri a century earlier had been instigated by the prophets Elijah and Elisha and supported by the founder of the puritan Rechabites. But the cruel and reckless bloodshed of Jehu's rebellion revolted Hosea as much as the religious practices of the dynasty against which Jehu rebelled; this is the meaning of the words: " I will visit the blood of Jezreel upon the house of Jehu " (Hos. 1: 4) . Hosea's lot was cast in an unsettled age when the kings of Israel had little to commend them. After the death of Jeroboam II in 743 B.C., there were six kings in twenty-eight years, only one of whom died a natural death, so full was the time of plots and counterplots and assassinations. Altogether, Hosea is brought to a point at which the monarchy seems an evil thing in itself, and an abandonment of Yahweh. That attitude is reflected in the later story of the origin of the kingship (found in I Sam. 8; 10: 17–24; 11: 12–15) , which represents it as a defection from Yahweh from the very beginning when it was condemned by Samuel. The origin of that quite inconsistent story seems to be Hosea's similar view of the monarchy, in the light of what it had come to mean for Israel. So he announces judgment on the royal house (Hos. 5: 1) , a party to contemporary evils (chs. 7: 3, 5; 9: 15) as well as the victim of them (chs. 7: 7; 10: 7) . His attitude is explicitly stated in the words: " They have set up kings, but not by me; they have made princes, and I knew it not " (ch. 8: 4) ; " I gave thee kings in my anger and took them away in my wrath " (ch. 13: 11) .

Besides all this, Hosea denounces those foreign relations which were so characteristic of the politics of the times. Israel lay between Assyria and Egypt, the plaything of both. Against the menace of Assyria, the only external refuge was Egypt. So there was a pro-Assyrian and a pro-Egyptian party, and between them the history of those days runs its troublous course. " Ephraim, he mixeth himself among the peoples: Ephraim is a half-baked cake " (ch. 7: 8) or " a silly dove " (v. 11) ; " they call unto Egypt, they go to Assyria." To Hosea, as to his contemporary in the south, Isaiah, the only true policy was no policy at all, but a penitent return to Yahweh, whose business it was to look after His recovered bride (ch. 2: 19 f.).

Such were the chief social and religious institutions of the time which the prophet condemned. They were to him the entrenchments of moral evil, at once expressing and reinforcing the " spirit of whoredom," the inner spirit of alienation from Yahweh, which he recognized as the real root of all the trouble, in the national as in the domestic tragedy of his experience.

3. *The Inner Alienation*

Hosea's phrase to describe the inner source of this externally visible alienation from God is " the spirit of whoredom." [1] It is obviously drawn from his own experience of Gomer's conduct, and denotes the actual impulse to sexual immorality which was at the root of her infidelity. In its figurative transference to Israel, it denotes the inner spirit which found outer expression in all the acts which Hosea has been seen to condemn. This is evident from the context of the two passages in which

[1] Cf. the spirit of perverseness (Isa. 19: 14) ; of uncleanness (Zech. 13: 2) ; and of jealousy (Num. 5: 14).

Hosea employs the phrase. In ch. 4: 12 he says that the spirit of whoredom has caused the people to wander away [1] from the true God, and he illustrates this by reference to divination by means of the sacred tree or the sacred staff, and to the sacrifice and incense offering upon the high places, with which sacred prostitution was connected, and also to the idolatry to which Ephraim was wedded (v. 17). All this was done in the name of Yahweh, but the prophet contends that it springs from a false conception of His nature and requirements; it is the lower passions of men which produce this actual immorality and this religious infidelity. In the second context (ch. 5: 4), the phrase is in parallelism with the words " they know not Yahweh." It is the opposite of the promise in ch. 2: 20, where the outcome of the new betrothal in righteousness and in justice, in loving-kindness and in mercies, is so described. To know Yahweh is to be just and loving; not to know him is to be the opposite, and this injustice and disloyalty spring from within. They seek God zealously, but do not find him, because they have this false idea of what he is and what he wants; he has withdrawn himself from such a false approach to him, and their very deeds themselves will forever prevent a true approach (ch. 5: 6).

This conception of sin as essentially consisting in an inner spirit which manifests itself in outer acts was something new in the history of religion, however familiar and obvious it has become to us. There is nothing in Amos, the immediate predecessor of Hosea, which goes as deep as this. The prophets generally gave a new moral content to sin, in place of the older idea of a broken taboo, and infringement of a nonmoral " holiness." But it was Hosea who penetrated to the genuinely

1 Like a lost animal (Ex. 23: 4) or a drunken man (Isa. 28: 7).

religious aspect of sin, as consisting in an alienated spirit. In this he is notably followed by Jeremiah, his spiritual kinsman in the south, a century and more after him. Jeremiah's prophecy of the new covenant is itself a transference of emphasis from the external act to the inner spirit, as the only sphere in which a right relation between man and God can be established. Third in the great line comes the Prophet of Nazareth, with the Sermon on the Mount, declaring that it is the lust within that is the essential sin, which he identifies with the outward act that expresses it.

To us it seems obvious that such a conception of sin individualizes it, and this, in fact, was seen by Jeremiah. It cannot be claimed that Hosea sees the full consequence of his own inner emphasis on the individual life. It is of the nation Israel, as a whole, that he is thinking, according to the sense of corporate personality which characterizes the thought of Israel. True, the deeds which he condemns are committed by individual persons, as his own experience of Gomer's conduct has amply shown. But it is the social mass of evil, the common stock to which each man contributes, that is primarily in his mind, and it is the common spirit, the spirit that prompts the whole people to such evil, which he discerns. We cannot speak of more than an implicit individualism in his phrase.

What shall we say, then, of the sense of individual responsibility for the evil? Here, also, the consequences of his insight are not drawn out by the prophet, in the manner of Ezekiel. In fact, there are distinct degrees of blame in the condemnations of Hosea. We have seen that his bitterest invective is directed against the priests, for their own misconduct and for their neglect of duty toward the people: " My people are destroyed for lack of knowledge; because thou hast rejected knowledge, I will also reject thee, that thou shalt be no priest to me " (ch. 4: 6). In such a differentiation of responsibility, we are near to the teaching of the Gospel: " that servant which knew his lord's will, and made not ready, nor did according to his will, shall be beaten with many stripes; but he that knew not, and did things worthy of stripes, shall be beaten with few stripes " (Luke 12: 47, 48). In every sin we commit, there is surely something of our own and something of the society in which we have grown up, and no human calculus is adequate to adjust the proportion of responsibility, though every man may come near to the knowledge of his own. The complexity of the assessment is all the more if we regard this earth as part of a larger order, as the Bible does, an order in which the good and evil of an invisible world play their part in influencing our conduct.

4. *The Atrophy of the Will*

That inner alienation of which we have been speaking is not only the source of evil deeds, it is also in increasing degree their consequence. This is one of the most subtle and most terrible aspects of sin, with which we are all familiar, an aspect that constantly recurs in literature. Writers who cannot be accused of theological prepossessions tell us as emphatically as they can that there is an atrophy of the will born of evil deeds. Here, for example, is Burns, speaking of sexual sin:

> I waive the quantum o' the sin,
> The hazard of concealing;
> But, och! it hardens a' within,
> And petrifies the feeling!

There is a deeply impressive story by Nathaniel Hawthorne, called *Ethan Brand*. It is the study of a man obsessed with the idea of the " unpardonable sin," who sets out on the quest of it, and finds it nowhere. He returns to his home, and finds it in his own heart — " The sin of an intellect that triumphed over the sense of brotherhood with man and reverence for God, and sacrificed everything to its own mighty claims." In the cold and unsympathetic quest, his own heart " had withered . . . had contracted . . . had hardened . . . had perished "! There is also a grim poem by Whittier, called " The Answer," all the more memorable when we remember the gentle spirit of the man who wrote it:

No word of doom may shut thee out,
No wind of wrath may downward whirl,
No swords of fire keep watch about
The open gates of pearl;

A tenderer light than moon or sun,
Than song of earth a sweeter hymn,
May shine and sound forever on,
And thou be deaf and dim.

Forever round the Mercy-seat
The guiding lights of Love shall burn;
But what if, habit-bound, thy feet
Shall lack the will to turn?

What if thine eye refuse to see,
Thine ear of Heaven's free welcome fail,
And thou a willing captive be,
Thyself thy own dark jail?

Does Hosea, then, say this? Not in so many words, but it is implicit in some of his sayings: " Whoredom and wine and new wine take away the will " (literally, " the heart," " the seat of volition ") (ch. 4: 11); " Ephraim is wedded to idols, let him alone " (v. 17); " Their doings will not suffer them to turn unto their God " (ch. 5: 4) ; " They became abominable like that which they loved (ch. 9: 10). Further, we may take his use of the figure of sowing and reaping as indicating the closeness of connection between the sin and its penalty, or some of its penalty. Thus, in ch. 10: 12, 13 he says:

> Sow to yourselves according to righteousness,
> Reap according to (your) piety. . . .
> Ye have ploughed wickedness,
> Ye have reaped injustice
> Ye have eaten the fruit of (your) lies.

This is an anticipation of Saint Paul's: " Whatsoever a man soweth, that shall he also reap "; and of Emerson's principle, in the great essay on *Compensation:* " Crime and punishment grow out of one stem. Punishment is a fruit that unsuspected ripens within the flower of the pleasure which concealed it." The figure doubtless implies much besides the moral atrophy of the sinner, since the Hebrew principle of retribution and its confinement within the limits of this life demanded an ultimate adjustment of outer circumstance to the inner quality of the man. But it includes that moral deterioration, a deterioration which is asserted by other prophets also. Isaiah at his call hears the words of commission in the enigmatic terms: " Make the heart of this people fat, and make their ears heavy, and shut their eyes; lest they see with their eyes, and hear with their ears, and their heart should understand and turn and be healed " (Isa.

43

6: 10) . Here, as we saw in the initial command to Hosea, the consequences are automatically included in the commission, but the underlying assumption is that the sequel of disobedience is the growing inability to obey. So also in well-known words, Jeremiah asks:

> Can the Ethiopian change his skin, or the leopard his spots?
> Then may ye also do good, that are trained to do evil (Jer. 13: 23) .

The Hebrew vocabulary for " sin " tells us the same thing. There are words that refer to some outer standard — such as those that speak of deviation from the right way; or the forfeiture of status that accompanies the judicial verdict of " guilty "; or an act of rebellion toward a superior, or of infidelity to an agreement — but there are a number of words also that characterize sin as " vice," i.e., as something that is bad in itself, before any external standard of judgment is applied. In this connection we may notice the striking figure of old age which is applied to Israel, the premature senility of the man who has abused his body: " Strangers have devoured his strength and he knoweth it not; yea, gray hairs are sprinkled upon him and he knoweth it not " (Hos. 7: 9) .

5. *Sin Against the Background of Grace*

Yet the truest and deepest revelation of the nature of sin does not come from its inner or outer consequences, but from its aspects when thrown up against the background of grace — the grace of God which has marked Israel's long history, and turns her present disposition and conduct into churlish ingratitude. Alike in the prophetic teaching of the Old Testament and in the apostolic teaching of the New, the sin of sins is ingratitude. That ingratitude is seen to its full extent only when God is conceived as the Father who has taught his little child to walk, and carried him when weary in his arms (ch. 11: 1 ff.) : " Though I have taught and strengthened their arms, yet do they imagine mischief against Me " (ch. 7: 15) ; " Though I would redeem them, yet have they spoken lies against Me " (v. 13). That again is a recurrent note in the greater prophets, and prepares for the New Testament. How striking an expression of this is found in Paul's experience, when praying in the Temple at the outset of his missionary work (Acts 22: 17). He sees two faces before him, the face of Stephen and the face of Christ. In that dramatic contrast of unforgotten sin and unforgettable grace, each is illuminated. If it is grace alone that can deal with the obdurate heart, so it is grace alone that reveals the sin of its obduracy. Gomer's infidelity takes on a new and darker color against the fidelity of Hosea's love; his cross, like that of a greater prophet, is the measure of human sin before it becomes the means of a divine salvation.

THE VICTORY OF GRACE

Hosea was not only the first discoverer of the inwardness of sin; he was also the pioneer of what may be called " evangelical realism." By this is meant that he fearlessly projected his own consciousness of a " gracious " attitude toward Gomer and his own experience of the cost of that grace into the consciousness of God. This projection, as we have seen, depends for its validity on the truth of the kinship of man and God; but if that is not in some sense true, we can say nothing at all about God. If it is true, then we dispose at once of the need for any transaction or legal fiction to reconcile God to man, since his love for man becomes our starting point. But we also get a much deeper conception of the cost of grace to God, and we get rid of any superficial idea of grace as simply divine benevolence. If it costs so much to a man like Hosea to be gracious to a sinner, what must it not cost to God? More than this, we see more clearly from the example of Hosea why the New Testament so constantly insists that the believer in God's grace must necessarily be a lover of his brethren. You cannot really believe in the grace of God unless you are confident in its ultimate victory; but you cannot have that confidence from the outside of things. Unless you believe in the victory of grace over sin in your human relations, you cannot have any confidence about it in the divine. Hosea acted as he did toward Gomer because he was sure that the way of grace was the way of ultimate victory. That assurance is paralleled in his faith that God would be victorious through grace over the sin and sinfulness of Israel.

This conviction was deepened by his corresponding insight into the inwardness of sin. Because the root of sin was the spirit of infidelity far deeper than any particular act which expressed it, the remedy for sin must be something not less deep and vital — the cleansing and liberating power of a new spirit which should replace the old, and could be created only by its like. Amos had taught that the inevitable reaction of a holy God to sin must be judgment and the infliction of penalty; Hosea, not excluding penalty, but transforming it into discipline, makes that reaction to consist primarily in the suffering of grace, through the love that will not let the sinner go. Only this deeper way of grace could be the way of victory, for it alone was really spiritual in principle, and able to deal with the things of the spirit of man. This is evangelical realism. Instead of superimposing a theological structure, true or false, upon the events of history, it goes deeper into those events to find their intrinsic nature and their cosmic significance, whether they relate to the human or the divine. As Blake puts it:

> God appears, and God is Light,
> To those poor souls who dwell in Night;
> But does a Human Form display
> To those who dwell in realms of Day.

In this way alone can we hope to bring out the true continuity of the Old Testament and the New which has welded them both into the Christian Bible. They are one, because they both find God *in* man, and both bring the God they find *to* man. They are one, because, whatever the difference of scale and scope, the grace of our

47

Lord Jesus Christ is of the same texture as the grace of the Prophet Hosea.

1. *The Initiative of Grace*

The first great characteristic of that attitude and act which we call " grace " is its spontaneity; it takes the initiative, without waiting for anything that could warrant it. Thus the Epistle to the Ephesians (Eph. 2: 4 ff.) declares that the exceeding riches of God's grace are shown through his initial action in Christ, with whom we are raised to new life: " By grace have you been saved through faith, and that [salvation] is not from yourselves — of God is the gift; not from works, that no one may boast." A notable passage by Karl Holl claims this quality of initiative as the chief characteristic of the Christian faith, the quality that distinguishes it from all other religions: " We may say that Jesus reverses the usual relation of religion and morality. Every other religion, at any rate every religion of higher aims, bases the personal relation of God on the right conduct of man. The more moral anyone is — understanding ' moral ' in the broadest sense, as including the cult — the nearer he stands to God. According to Jesus, it is, on the contrary, God who makes a beginning; it is He who posits a new thing in forgiveness. From it, however, there arises a real, close and warm relation to God, and at the same time a morality that can dare to take God Himself as its exemplar " (*Urchristentum und Religionsgeschichte,* p. 22).

This quality of spontaneity is not denied by recognizing the real bond that unites God to man. Such bond can be of a lower or a higher kind. At the lowest level, it can indeed be conceived as the bargaining which we

48

have just set in contrast with grace. At the higher, however, it springs from the compulsion of love, i.e., from the very nature of God himself. This, surely, is *his* perfect freedom, to be able to be nothing but what he is. Thus, his covenant with Israel, on which the whole conception of Israel's religion rests, is not, for the prophets, a bargain at all. Amos repudiates the popular idea that Yahweh is mechanically bound to Israel as its God, and lifts the relation to the moral level. Hosea does far more; he lifts it to the level of the highest human relationships, viz., marriage and parenthood. He penetrates to that spirit of love which alone can fulfill the bond of the letter. For such a man, the covenant (*berith;* Hos. 2: 18; 6: 7; 8: 1) is the shell of which " loving-kindness " (*hesed;* chs. 2: 19; 4: 1; 6: 4, 6; 10: 12; 12: 6) is the kernel. That great word " *hesed* " is very difficult to render, for it expresses the moral bondage of love, the loving discharge of an admitted obligation, the voluntary acceptance of a responsibility. It is significant that Amos does not use the term at all, whilst it occurs six times in Hosea. Its finest expression is in ch. 11: 8, 9:

> How shall I give thee up, Ephraim?
> How shall I deliver thee up, Israel?
> How shall I make thee as Admah?
> How shall I set thee as Zeboim?
> Mine heart is turned within me,
> My compassions are kindled together.
> I will not execute the fierceness of mine anger,
> I will not return to destroy Ephraim.

That is the fundamental fact in the relation of God to Israel; he cannot let her go because he is what he is. He took the initiative with her, long ago, from the land of Eygpt (ch. 13: 4) ; now, in her need, he takes a new ini-

49

tiative, like the old (ch. 2: 14–23). His first delight in his adopted child was as that of one who finds grapes in the wilderness, or the first-ripe fig (ch. 9: 10); but as a result of the new initiative, he can say, "From Me is thy fruit found" (ch. 14: 8). The terms of the new invitation are clearly expressed both at the beginning and the end of Hosea's prophecies: "I will betroth thee unto Me for ever; yea I will betroth thee unto Me in righteousness, and in justice and in loving-kindness and in mercies. I will even betroth thee unto Me in faithfulness: and thou shalt know Yahweh" (ch. 2: 19, 20); "I will heal their backsliding, I will love them freely: for Mine anger is turned away from him" (ch. 14: 4).

This, then, is the gospel according to Hosea. It is expressed, like that of the Prophet of Nazareth, in deeds as well as words; in fact, for both, it is true to say that the deed is the essential word, which the spoken syllables can only report. The symbolic act of the prophet, most of all when it moves on so high a level and involves such human relations as that of Hosea, becomes the very word of God. "I have spoken unto the prophets, and I have multiplied visions, and by the ministry of the prophets have I used similitudes" (ch. 12: 10). The first preaching of the cross, for Hosea as well as for Jesus, is the cross itself. In both, the personal initiative, under moral compulsion alone, is made evident; in both, the visible deed is made the witness and token to the invisible reality: "Go yet, love a woman beloved of her friend and an adultress, even as Yahweh loveth the children of Israel, though they turn unto other gods"; "God commendeth His own love toward us, in that, while we were yet sinners, Christ died for us" (Hos. 3: 1; Rom. 5: 8).

2. *The Redemptive Work of Grace*

Can we carry further the analogy, or as I prefer to say, the intrinsic relation between the cross of Hosea and the cross of Christ? Can we go on to speak of the redemptive work of Hosea in relation to Gomer, with the full consciousness that we find in it something akin to the redemptive work of Christ? Let us look more closely at what is recorded in the third chapter of Hosea. He tells us that he had to purchase her, perhaps from the slavery of sanctuary prostitution, at a slave's ransom. The price was fifteen pieces of silver, and a homer and a half of barley, which is thought to be the equivalent of the thirty shekels at which a male or female slave was rated in Hebrew law (Ex. 21: 32). Given the circumstances, this was obviously a necessary step in the process of her recovery. Yet it is an accidental element in the redemptive work, which was essentially spiritual. The Salvation Army, on occasion, have purchased Chinese girls at 30 s. a head, from their parents, in order to save them from a life of shame. But the really redemptive work was in the purpose to train these girls under Christian influences to a life of virtue. The act of grace was in the intention which informed the visible deed. So we should rightly say of Hosea that his purpose to save Gomer, by whatever means, was the essential expression of grace. The price paid for the execution of that purpose was spiritual rather than material, though the two are never wholly separated in our mingled life of body and soul. The spiritual price can be measured only in terms of suffering. When a holy will takes to itself and accepts the burden of responsibility for an unholy will, there is the inevitable condition that the sin is transformed in the consciousness of the holy man into suffering; he cannot share its burden on any other terms. There is the suffering of actual contact with it, which Henry Drummond experienced as the repulsion of a cleanly person from physical filth; there is the suffering of inward association as well as the shame and disgrace which outward association may bring. There is the suffering which the very etymology of the word " patience " suggests, the struggle against disappointment and disillusionment and the temptation to abandon a hopeless quest. There is the sacrifice of so much that might have been but for this perhaps thankless task. All these and more will be known to anyone who has honestly tried to redeem a life with which he owns solidarity and for which he accepts responsibility. The holier he is, the more will be his suffering. This is the constant law of holy grace, whether in man or God. Because it is grace, it cannot stand aloof and disclaim association with the sinner; because it is holy, it can associate itself with him only on terms of suffering.

All that is true of Jesus, in his own far greater way. However we are to conceive his redemptive work, that work was wrought out essentially through spiritual sufferings, whilst their physical accompaniments are little more than the occasion or expression of the spiritual. Would not the daily association with the alienated spirit of Judas be a crown of thorns to Him far more painful than that he wore in the judgment hall? Was not Gethsemane his real Calvary? The best of us can get but a glimpse now and then of what it means to be holy with and among sinners, who yet may not be disowned and avoided. But we cannot say these things of Jesus and call them part of his redemptive work without recognizing the similarity of his experience with the saints of God before and after him at whatever lower level. Whatever is intrinsically true of the redemptive suffering of Jesus must be true in its own degree of all the suffering of holy grace, such as is before us in Hosea's experience.

In what sense, then, can all such holy suffering be called redemptive in the full sense? That is, not simply as constituting a pathetic appeal to the sinner, powerful and essential as that appeal must be, but as " atoning " for the sin. There are two distinct aspects of it. There is the actual transformation of the evil of suffering (for suffering is an evil) in the saint; the transformation which makes the voluntary acceptance of that suffering an act of grace, full of gracious beauty. This transformation is quite distinct from the possible transformation of the sinner himself, of which we shall have to speak later. Whether or not that takes place, this is secure; an ugly thing has been made beautiful. All sin is ugly, and all grace is graceful, when the sin is sin and the grace is grace. (Here we note in passing a hint of ultimate reconciliation between the aesthetic and the ethical standards and interests.) As we look at the ugliness of Gomer's sin passing into the consciousness of Hosea to be transformed into a beauty that anticipates that of the Gospel, shall we not say that one element of atonement is present? We can never justify sin by its results; but this is the reversal of those results, the creation of a new spiritual gain that far transcends the loss incurred by the sin.

The other aspect, the other element in the atoning work of holy suffering, is raised when we ask what is the worth of this value to God. How does it concern him that the suffering of the saint can thus transform evil into good? If we speak anthropomorphically, we can say that it is a sacrifice with which he is well pleased, an offering that is the truest worship, since it is the fullest recognition of his holy worth. But directly we try to work out our anthropomorphic metaphors, such as sacrifice, ransom, vicarious penalty, into some sort of theory, we get into difficulties. They are true, or they express a truth, in showing that the sinner cannot atone for his own sin. They are false whenever they suggest such a real gulf between man and God as has to be bridged by means external to Himself, or such an attitude of alienation as demands propitiation before He is gracious. But there is a deeper view, however impossible it be to rationalize or systematize it. If a prophet can identify himself with God, so that he suffers with the suffering of God over the sin of Israel, how much more will it be true that God suffers in the suffering of his prophets? The actuality of their suffering is part of his suffering; their crosses are gathered up into one great cross for him; the spiritual values they achieve are his, through that intimate and inexpressible union of God and his saints, imperfect in them, but perfected in his Son. He is what Isaiah calls him, the great burden bearer (Isa. 46: 1–4), because in him we live and move and have our being; because he is immanent as well as transcendent. In the mystery of man's life within God, sinner or saint, God bears the sin through suffering, and shares the burden with his saints. If we have rightly understood the story of Hosea's life, he not only appeals to Gomer by the declaration of his unbroken love, but tries to help her practically toward recovery of her lost place. But he does more than this; he suffers with her and for her. Indeed, it may be said quite properly that he suffers far more than she can, just because of his forgiving love. Shall we not say, with Professor H. R.

Mackintosh, that the forgiveness of God "must prove as full, as unqualified and overpowering in generosity, as the forgiveness of good men "? In man, as in God, true forgiveness *costs* something. Its measure may be partly seen in the attempt of the good man to raise the fallen, as a real element in his forgiveness. But behind the visible acts of helpfulness and reconciliation, there is an inner cost, a suffering born from sacrificial love, a suffering greater in the saint than in the sinner, and surely greatest in God. Thus we may speak, with Bushnell, of "a cross in God before the wood is seen upon Calvary" (*The Vicarious Sacrifice,* Charles Scribner's Sons, 1866, p. 73). To identify the atonement ultimately with the sacrificial love of God is not to minimize in the least the significance of the cross of Christ in history, for that becomes the supreme actualization in time of the truth that holds for all eternity. But this way of facing the doctrine of atonement does remove it from the category of a transaction, a mere event, a sort of device belonging to the "plan of salvation." Atonement now becomes something deep-based in the very nature of God, as natural to him as the forgiving love of a human saint. If it be true that in God we live and move and have our being, then our sins must somehow be conceived within the circle of his holiness. Yet how can they be conceived there save as suffering within the Godhead — suffering for man, penal, disciplinary, chastening; and suffering for God, sacrificial, redemptive; and, at last, transformed into the joy of triumph? We should like to know whether the suffering love of Hosea did avail to win back the sinning Gomer, but, whether it did or not, that suffering love has transformed a sordid story into a prophecy of the Gospel. Similarly, the sacrificial love of God is always faced by the mystery of human personality and freedom, and none can declare the issue of its appeal to the individual; but the love behind it transforms the meaning of the world's history and makes it glorious with the " iridescent " wisdom of God (Eph. 3: 10).

3. *The Discipline of Grace*

When the inwardness of Israel's sin was under consideration, our thought was confined to the inward penalty, that atrophy of the spirit of man which sin inevitably induces. This essential separation from God is always the real penalty of sin. But the external and visible penalty occupies a large part of the prophecies of Hosea. Under many figures he describes the wrath of God against sin, and the penalty which falls on it. Yahweh is compared with the lion, the leopard, and the bear that attacks the defenseless prey (Hos. 13: 7, 8), or the fowler who snares the bird in his net (ch. 7: 12) or the destroying moth (ch. 5: 12). The doom of Israel is represented as inexorable: " Shall I ransom them from the power of Sheol? Shall I redeem them from death? O death where are thy plagues? O Sheol where is thy destruction? " (ch. 13: 14). The exact nature of this destruction is again made clear in numerous passages. It is war and invasion and all the sufferings they bring, whether from Assyria or from Egypt, the two great powers on the horizon, and it will end in exile: " Ephraim shall return to Egypt, and they shall eat unclean food in Assyria " (ch. 9: 3); " They shall be wanderers among the nations " (v. 17); " The Assyrian shall be his king " (ch. 11: 5); " Egypt shall gather them up " (ch. 9: 6). It is immaterial to the prophet whether the destruction come from Assyria or Egypt; he is not concerned with foretelling events, like an *Old Moore's Almanac,* but with declaring the certain and inevitable penalty of sin, in the shame and desolation, the disorder and helplessness, the utter overthrow of all the strong places in which the nation trusted (chs. 10: 14; 11: 6). He may have witnessed the harrowing scenes of the deportation of 732 B.C.

Yet we should miss the real meaning of these prophecies of judgment, if we forgot what we have already emphasized — the divine purpose to save. The penalty is certain, but only if the sin endures. Yahweh has withdrawn himself, but only " till they have borne their guilt and seek My face " (ch. 5: 15). The individual members of the nation are bidden to plead with their mother, the nation, in its corporate personality: " lest I strip her naked " (ch. 2: 3). The final chapter visualizes a genuine repentance and return, in which the nation seeks healing from him who has smitten (ch. 6: 1; cf. ch. 14: 4). It is clear, therefore, that the penalty is meant to be pedagogic; it is intended to secure repentance, and cannot be rightly estimated as mere retribution, though its retributive aspect is so strongly emphasized. Even as penalty, it falls within the covenant of grace, and gets its meaning from the ultimate purpose of God.

We must beware, then, here, as whenever such themes are discussed, lest we deny or minimize the reality of the wrath of God against sin, or conceive of that wrath as propitiated by the smoking altars and the costly gifts. That is what the ordinary Israelite thought, but it is the very thing which the greater prophets condemned. They were struggling to express their conviction that divine retribution is a reality, carried out according to moral principles. That is true for Amos; but Hosea, without any abandonment of it, proclaims a higher morality of

" loving-kindness." The result of this is that penalty may be transformed into discipline. That is what it certainly is in the purpose of God; that is what it must surely become in all who turn to him, i.e., who come to share in his purpose. We need not ask whether the retributive element is exact — the problem that troubled Israelite thinkers so greatly in the later days, when the corporate personality of the nation was modified by a new individualism, which asked how the individual experience could be shown to be one of exact retribution. In Hosea's time, the nation is the unit, and the later problem has not emerged. If one generation does not see the work of Yahweh, then another will; that suffices.

The really important aspect of penalty is its potential effect on the sinner who encounters it — a truth which need not and ought not to hide from us that some penalties are inexorable, even in the course of an outward order of events. Thus, a nation that has gone so far down the slippery slope of civil strife, conspiracy, and disorder as Israel could hardly have escaped from Assyria, however ardent its repentance; a woman who had fallen like Gomer could never recover her innocence. The point that must not be missed is that a true repentance which enters into God's purpose will accept the penalty that continues after such repentance, but will transform it into willingly accepted discipline. This is the implicit hope behind Hosea's treatment of Gomer in chapter 2, when she is separated for the " many days " of discipline, before the old relations with her husband can be resumed. This is what the great prophet of the Exile learned so well, when he bade his fellow countrymen consecrate their sufferings into a sacrificial offering, through which the nations of the world might be not only moved to penitence but also enabled to approach

God through the sacrifice. The unit of experience is always the outer event plus the inner attitude; for the outer event has meaning only in the light of that inner attitude, and that inner attitude has power to transform the worst into the best.

4. *The Response to Grace*

Finally, we have to consider the victory of grace in the heart of the penitent sinner, the culminating point of the whole appeal and work of grace. Here, it can be said that, " The great teacher at once of the necessity and the value of true repentance was Hosea, who dwelt upon it positively, as though no more was needed " (Welch, *Post-Exilic Judaism,* p. 301). The reference of the " no more " in this sentence is to the cult, and its context makes a contrast with Isaiah and Micah, who " developed the theme with a conscious reference to the demands of the cult." Hosea's attitude is most concisely expressed in the words quoted on two occasions by Jesus, viz.: " I delight in mercy and not in sacrifice; and the knowledge of God more than burnt-offerings " (ch. 6: 6; cf. Matt. 9: 13; 12: 7). Here the word rendered " mercy " (*hesed*) can mean either piety toward God or kindness toward man, and perhaps includes both here. The sentence does not necessarily form a condemnation of the cult, any more than its quotation by Jesus implied this (cf. Mark 1: 44); but it does imply a very different emphasis, and the primary need of repentance manifested in changed conduct. This true and deep repentance is contrasted with the superficial and inadequate repentance described in the previous verses of the chapter: " Come and let us return unto Yahweh." Those who say this are less concerned with their sin than with their afflictions, and are quite sure that the mere appeal to God who had smitten them will produce an instant change of attitude in him; and that his favor and help are as certain as tomorrow's dawn, or as the autumnal and spring rains. With great artistic effect, the prophet reveals Yahweh taking up these comparisons by two others which represent the fickleness of the " piety " offering this so-called repentance: " Your piety is as the morning cloud, and as the night-mist that goeth early away." We might compare its superficiality with that of the dying Heine's jest: *" Dieu me pardonnera; c'est son métier."* With this is purposely contrasted that fine expression of a true and lasting penitence which the prophet puts by anticipation in the mouth of Israel. This liturgy of the confession of sin and of the declaration of grace has been rightly made the culminating point of the book (Hos., ch. 14). It begins with the prophet's invitation, and his appeal to the discipline of experience (ch. 1). Then he frames for Israel the words in which the evil of the old paths may be confessed, making articulate their inarticulate needs, which now replace the former glib approach to God. The " fruit of their lips " is still what they offer (ch. 2, R.V. margin), but it is now a true offering, for it is marked by definite and actual renunciation of the false helps and material aids of the past: " Asshur shall not save us; we will not ride upon horses: neither will we say any more to the work of our hands, Ye are our gods " (ch. 3). So comes the answer of grace: " I will heal. . . . I will love them freely " (ch. 4). The restored prosperity of Israel is described in figures of natural beauty (ch. 14: 5–7), and there is a closing antiphony in which Ephraim cries, " What have I to do any more with idols? " and Yahweh replies, " I have answered, and will regard him "; Ephraim declares,

" I am like a green fir tree "; and Yahweh gives what is at once a warning and a promise, " From Me is thy fruit found." It would be difficult to find in the whole Bible a truer program of penitence and grace expressed in their interaction.

But all this raises the important question: " What is to secure this deep and actual penitence, whether in Gomer or in the nation of which she is a representative product? The two parts of the question are one. Nor are we to unite them simply as though Gomer were an external object lesson of grace, to which the prophet could point and say, " God's attitude toward Israel is like this of mine toward Gomer." True as that would be to his conception, it would not at all adequately express its inner logic. We have to think here, as so often, of that category of corporate personality which is always conditioning the status of the individual in Biblical times. Gomer is more than what *we* mean by a symbol; she is for the time being the epitome of Israel. In her centers and culminates (for the prophet) the physical sexuality and the spiritual infidelity of Israel; in her, if his appeal of love be not in vain, will be found the first fruits of the new harvest, the promise and potency of a genuine repentance. The conversion of Gomer will be an actual event, part of, and instrumental to, the conversion of Israel. The symbolical acts of the prophets have, all of them, in greater or less degree, this quality of not merely *representing* the whole act of God, but of being a veritable part of it. If we say that this belongs to a stage of thought at which there was a defective sense of individual personality, that is true enough; yet such a stage may serve to show a real truth about the solidarity of the race, which the sheer individualism of modern times may easily miss. This is the counterpoise to the obvious weakness of appealing to a whole nation for what must be a series of individual repentances. Hosea's appeal is both individual and national, because *his first objective in Gomer is both.* Thus, the remembrance of this important category of ancient thought removes the apparent artificiality of making a domestic sorrow into a prophetic symbol, restores the actuality of life to the whole conduct and message of the prophet, and points forward to that death unto sin and resurrection unto life, which Paul saw as wrought out for us all in Christ.

Even so, how pathetic does the frailty of the appeal seem, when matched against the vested interests and the settled habits of a people, in which each sinning individual is entrenched, as Gomer was! From the standpoint of reason, the preaching of such a prophet was as much foolishness as the cross — because it was of the same nature. It is a spiritual appeal that matches itself in quixotic romance against all these things; but its strength is that it *is* spiritual, and alone able to grapple with the spiritual fact of the inwardness of sin. A Jew has put into the mouth of a Jew the words: " Christianity is Judaism run divinely mad " (Zwangwill, *Dreamers of the Ghetto,* p. 324). Certainly, there is real continuity with the Gospel in the evangelical appeal of Hosea. It is an impossible one, except for those who believe in the power of love; for those who so believe with all their heart and soul, it is the only possible appeal. A magistrate told me of a striking example of this. One Saturday, he had before him a girl charged with solicitation. He pleaded with her to abandon her dreadful trade, but in vain, though he offered to arrange for a new start in life for her. Finally, he adjourned the case till Monday. On Sunday, something moved him to write a letter to her, and with it he sent a bunch of flowers.

62

Some time after both had been delivered, the wardress entered the cell and found the girl lying on the floor and sobbing bitterly. All she would say was, " He sent me flowers, he sent me flowers." On Monday she was docile and ready to try again, and, as the years proved, not in vain.

One more question may be asked. What is the relation of the inner to the outer restoration? How far is true repentance accompanied by the full return of prosperity? The promises of Hosea are quite definite; he anticipates that the new betrothal (ch. 2: 19 ff.) will be followed by such harmony of outer nature as will supply all Israel's physical needs. In what we should call a series of cause and effect, the appeal of Israel is passed on by the corn and wine and oil to the earth from which they spring, and from the earth to the heavens that give the fertilizing and necessary rains; and from the heavens to Him who controls their storehouses, and who promises to respond to the appeal. Here, as in the epilogue to Job, the destiny of men must be wrought out, and the divine righteousness vindicated, in the visible life of earth, since there is no horizon of real life beyond death. The extension of that horizon to include the unseen, as in the Christian hope of immortality, provides an ampler arena for that vindication. At long last, the righteousness, which, for Hosea, includes the loving-kindness of God, must be fully vindicated; and forgiveness must be made visible, and reconciliation demonstrated. We may remember that such a hope enters into Paul's vision, when he speaks of the whole creation groaning and travailing in pain together until now, waiting for its deliverance from the bondage of corruption (Rom. 8: 21, 22). So, in society, it is as impossible to divorce the vision of a Kingdom of God on earth from the life and activities of the saints, as it is to limit their lives and activities by such a Kingdom. All we dare to say is that grace must be victorious in every realm, the earthly and the heavenly. Whatever happens in the future pilgrimage of man's spirit, the essential things must depend on the inner attitude, creative of the meaning of all that befalls it. The gospel of Hosea is that of a love able to transform life by creating a new attitude within, leading to a new interpretation of all things without, a new meaning. For spiritual beings, all that ultimately matters is the meaning of things, and man's spirit is capable of any miracle of transformation, when once aroused to its task. The great idea of love must be wrought out in life to become actual and so effective. It was made actual first through the cross of Hosea; it culminated in the cross of Christ, and it is continued in the countless other crosses of God's prophets and apostles in all generations.